INTRODUCING...

HANSEL & GRETEL

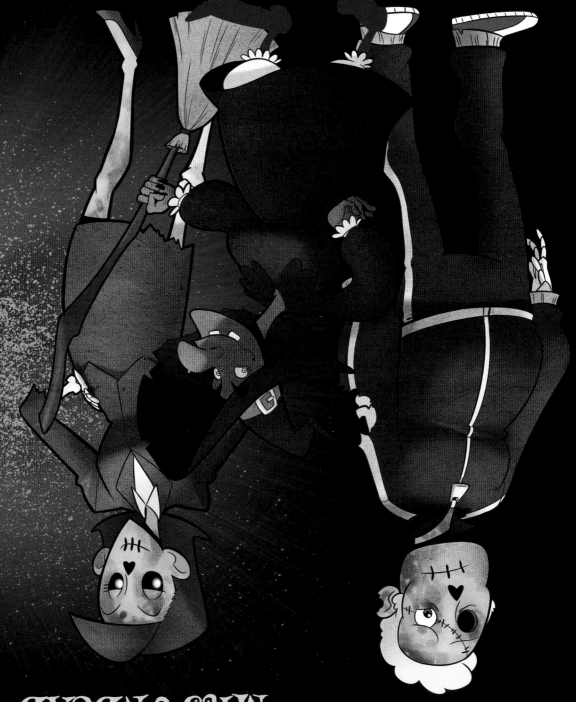

MS WITCH

MRS UNDEAD

MR UNDEAD

Raintree is an imprint of Capstone
Global Library Limited, a company
incorporated in England and Wales
having its registered office at 7
Pilgrim Street, London, EC4V 6LB –
Registered company number: 6695582

www.raintree.co.uk
myorders@raintree.co.uk

Text © Capstone Global Library
Limited 2016
The moral rights of the proprietor
have been asserted.

Edited by Sean Tulien
Designed by Hilary Wacholz
Original illustrations © Capstone 2016
Illustrated by Fernando Cano

ISBN 978 1 4747 1029 9 (paperback)
20 19 18 17 16
10 9 8 7 6 5 4 3 2 1

British Library Cataloguing in
Publication Data: a full catalogue
record for this book is available
from the British Library.

FAR OUT FAIRY TALES

HANSEL & GRETEL & ZOMBIES

A GRAPHIC NOVEL

BY BENJAMIN HARPER

ILLUSTRATED BY FERNANDO CANO

Once upon a time, in a distant corner of the Magical Forest...

...There was a lifeless graveyard.

CEMETERY

It had long been abandoned. No one had been buried there in years. No one visited.

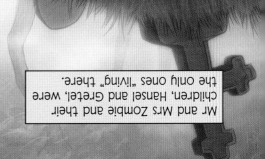

Mr and Mrs Zombie and their children, Hansel and Gretel, were the only ones "living" there.

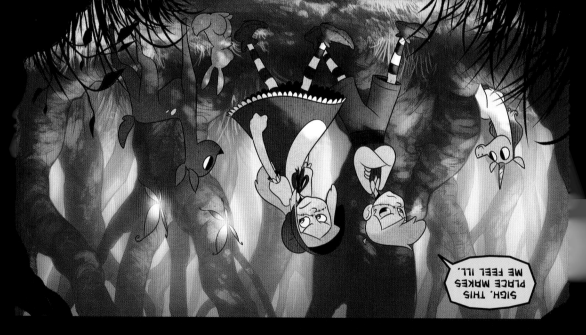

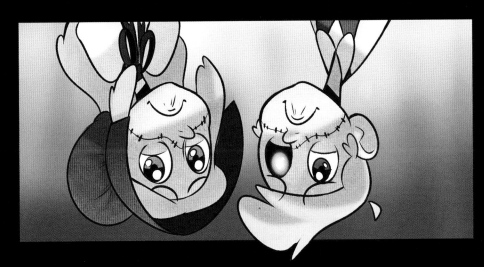

This is a full-page comic with the following text in speech bubbles and sound effects:

Panel 1:
- WHAT DO YOU THINK IT IS?
- I DON'T KNOW! BUT IT SMELLS *AWFUL.*

Panel 2:
- IT SEEMS TO BE SOME SORT OF... FOOD.

Panel 3:
- Why, whatever is the matter with those children?
- What kind of child doesn't like sweets!

Panel 4:
- HELLO? WE ARE EVER SO LOST AND VULNERABLE!
- Sigh. It seems I'm going to have to play the part if I want my dinner any time soon...
- *POOF*

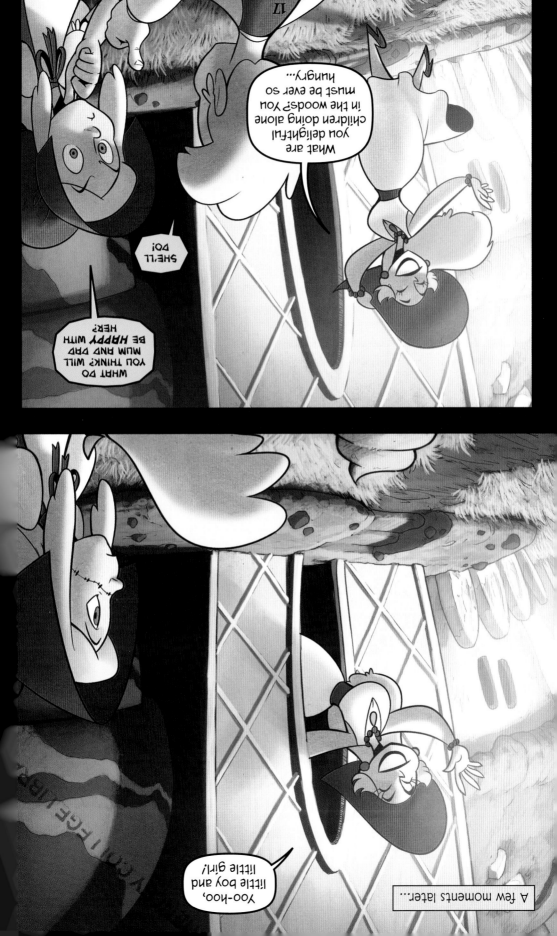

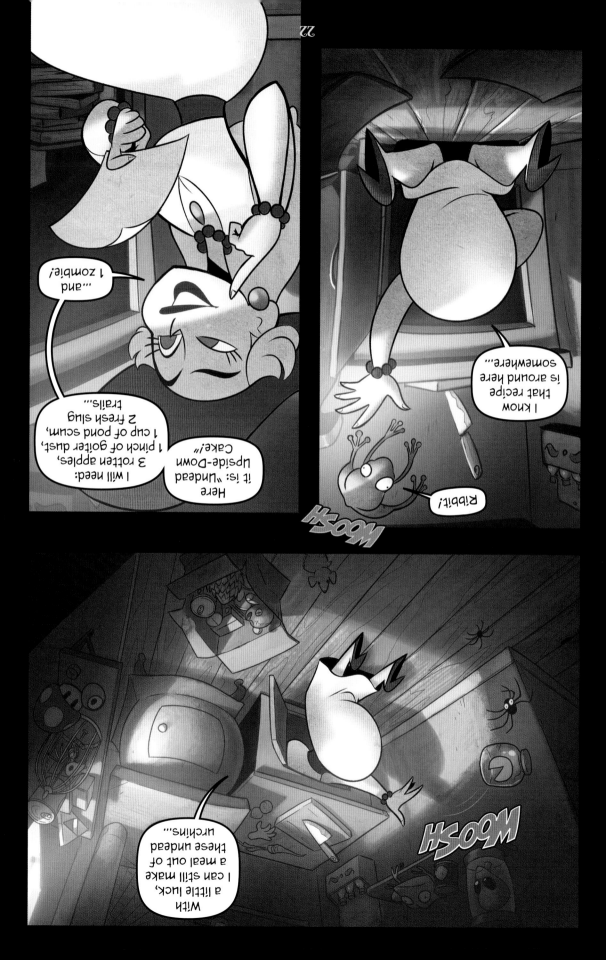

Gretel fixed the Witch's electrical wiring...

No!

I'M SO *FULL*...CAN'T *GRETEL* HAVE SOME NOW?

Keep eating!

...while Hansel ate and ate and ate.

Gretel mowed the lawn...

NOM NOM NOM

...while Hansel continued to eat.

...so she wracked her undead brain for a way out.

Gretel had a feeling her fate would be similar to her brother's if she climbed inside...

Fine. Get in there and light the oven, then.

OOF!!!

KICK!

SNATCH!

Oh, fine. Get out of the way, you braindead brat.

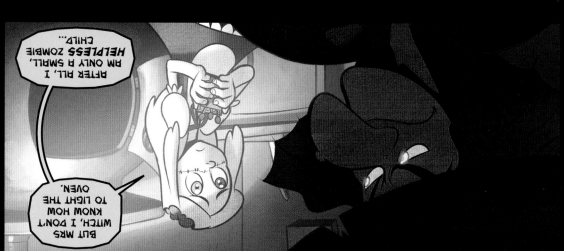

BUT MRS WITCH, I DON'T KNOW HOW TO LIGHT THE OVEN.

AFTER ALL, I AM ONLY A SMALL, *HELPLESS* ZOMBIE CHILD...

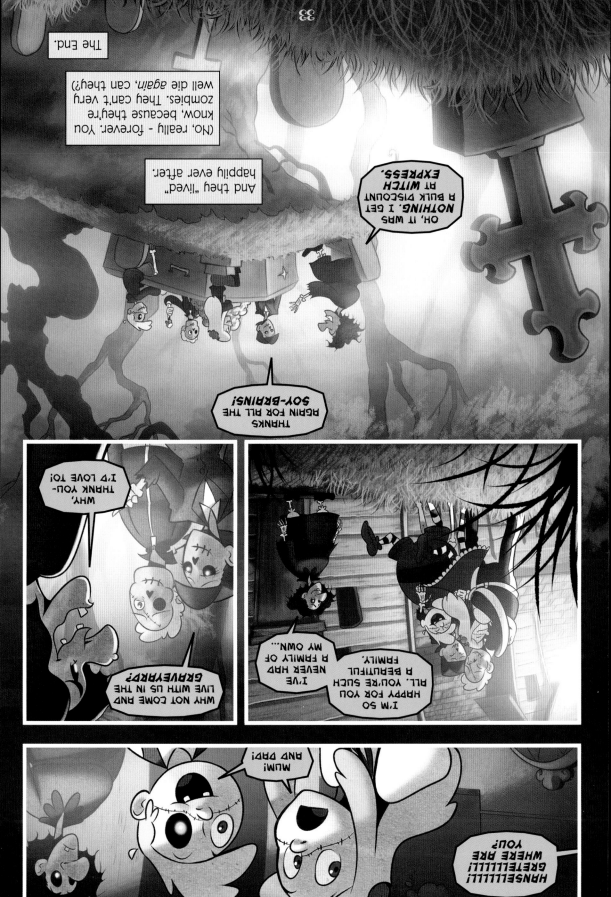

ALL ABOUT THE ORIGINAL TALE!

Zombies didn't appear in the original Brothers Grimm version of "Hansel and Gretel". However, Hansel and Gretel's parents were pretty monstrous.

You see, they tried not once – but twice – to abandon their children in the forest so they couldn't return home. The parents succeeded the second time, leaving Hansel and Gretel lost in the woods. In fact, their mother was so monstrous that she led them even further into the woods, ensuring they would never find their way home.

Lost and alone in the woods, Hansel and Gretel wandered aimlessly until they felt the need to lay down and sleep. Several days passed like this, until they became so hungry they could scarcely bear it. However, they soon came upon a strange sight: a house's walls made entirely of gingerbread, and the roof was made of cakes and other sweets.

The siblings, desperately hungry at this point, started eating the gingerbread house. Soon, the house's owner spotted them and welcomed them inside. To their surprise, the woman turned out to be a hungry witch who eats children!

The witch plumped up Hansel, hoping to make him nice and fat so he would be a bigger meal for her to eat. Meanwhile, the witch forced Gretel to work – and fed her nothing but crab shells.

One morning, the witch told Gretel to climb inside the hot oven to see if it was warm enough to bake bread. Gretel knew the witch was up to something, so she asked her to climb inside instead – and kicked the witch into the oven. She was never seen again.

Gretel freed her brother. In a room next to the kitchen, they found boxes of precious gems! When they finally found their way home, they discovered their father alone. While they'd been gone, their evil mother had died. Gretel pulled open her apron, releasing all the gems. The three of them lived richly and happily ever after.

A **FAR OUT** GUIDE TO HANSEL & GRETEL'S TALE TWISTS!

Two innocent, human siblings star in the original tale. In this version, they're zombies!

Hansel & Gretel get nabbed by the witch when they nibble her house. Zombie Hansel & Gretel get kidnapped because they *won't* eat the sweetie-house!

In the original tale, a witch tries to eat the children, but they burn her to cinders. (Yikes!) In this book, Zombie Gretel bites the witch, transforming her into one of them!

In the Brothers Grimm version of the story, the mother and the witch die. But in this far out version, everyone lives happily ever after – even the witch!

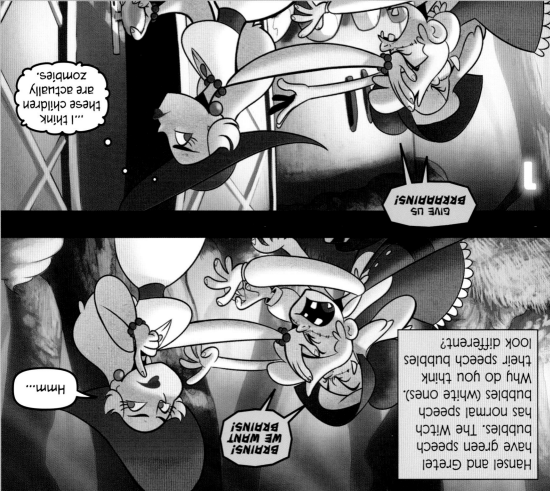

3

WELL, HUSBAND? WHAT DO YOU THINK?

THEY LOOK HORRIFYING! GREAT WORK, MY DEAR.

Why did Mr Undead say his children look "horrifying" when they are dressed up like normal human children?

IDEA!

4

5

I'VE GOT IT!

The word "IDEA!" is a sound effect, or SFX. Find a few SFX in this book. How are they used differently? Which SFX is your favourite?

Why is there a broken light bulb over Mrs Undead's head? What does it mean?

AUTHOR

Benjamin Harper has worked as an editor at Lucasfilm LTD. and DC Comics. He currently works at Warner Bros. Consumer Products in California, USA. He has written many books, including *Obsessed with Star Wars* and *Thank you, Superman!*

ILLUSTRATOR

Fernando Cano is an illustrator born in Mexico City, Mexico. He currently resides in Monterrey, Mexico, where he makes a living as an illustrator and colourist. He has done work for Marvel, DC Comics and role-playing games like Pathfinder from Paizo Publishing. In his spare time, he enjoys hanging out with friends, singing, rowing and drawing!

GLOSSARY

abandoned left behind without protection or care

character if someone is playing a character, they pretend to be someone other than who they are

goitre swelling on the front of the neck

horrifying causing someone to feel horror, shock or upset

journey act of travelling from one place to another, often to an undetermined location

soy soybeans and the food products that are made from soybeans. Many vegetarian foods are made from soy.

undead no longer alive but still able to move around

urchins old-fashioned name for children that are poor, dirty, annoying or likely to cause trouble

vulnerable easily hurt or harmed physically, mentally or emotionally

zombie dead person who is able to move because of magical means

FAR OUT FAIRY TALES

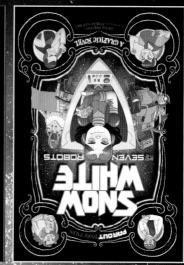

AWESOMELY EVER AFTER.